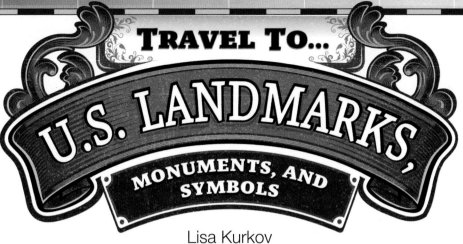

TRAVEL TO...
U.S. LANDMARKS,
MONUMENTS, AND SYMBOLS

Lisa Kurkov

HISTORIC
ROUTE
66

Rourke™

Before Reading: *Building Background Knowledge and Vocabulary*

Building background knowledge can help children process new information and build upon what they already know. Before reading a book, it is important to tap into what children already know about the topic. This will help them develop their vocabulary and increase their reading comprehension.

Questions and Activities to Build Background Knowledge:

1. Look at the front cover of the book and read the title. What do you think this book will be about?
2. What do you already know about this topic?
3. Take a book walk and skim the pages. Look at the table of contents, photographs, captions, and bold words. Did these text features give you any information or predictions about what you will read in this book?

Vocabulary: *Vocabulary Is Key to Reading Comprehension*

Use the following directions to prompt a conversation about each word:

- Read the vocabulary words.
- What comes to mind when you see each word?
- What do you think each word means?

Vocabulary Words:
- abolitionist
- Black Lives Matter
- controversial
- ecosystem
- escarpment
- genocide
- incarceration camps
- invasive species
- mesas
- parapets
- resiliency
- roadside attractions

During Reading: *Reading for Meaning and Understanding*

To achieve deep comprehension of a book, children are encouraged to use close reading strategies. During reading, it is important to have children stop and make connections. These connections result in deeper analysis and understanding of a book.

 Close Reading a Text

During reading, have children stop and talk about the following:

- Any confusing parts
- Any unknown words
- Text to text, text to self, text to world connections
- The main idea in each chapter or heading

Encourage children to use context clues to determine the meaning of any unknown words. These strategies will help children learn to analyze the text more thoroughly as they read.

When you are finished reading this book, turn to page 46 for Text-Dependent Questions and an Extension Activity.

TABLE of CONTENTS

LANDMARKS
& MONUMENTS

Golden Gate Bridge

Landmarks and monuments are often places that are immediately recognizable. You may have seen them on a poster or calendar, in your history book, on a TV show, or even in person. But what makes them important? They might have historical importance, like the Lincoln Memorial in Washington, DC, or they might be the site of an event, like the Alamo in San Antonio, where a major battle in the Texas Revolution took place.

As a culture and a society, we give meaning to these slabs of stone, sculpted metals, forests, temples, and roads. They remind us of who we are as a country, who we admire, what we've lost, and what we aspire to. Of course, these things are not the same for everyone; America is a diverse and complicated country.

California Redwood Trees

United States Capitol Building

Cape Hatteras Lighthouse

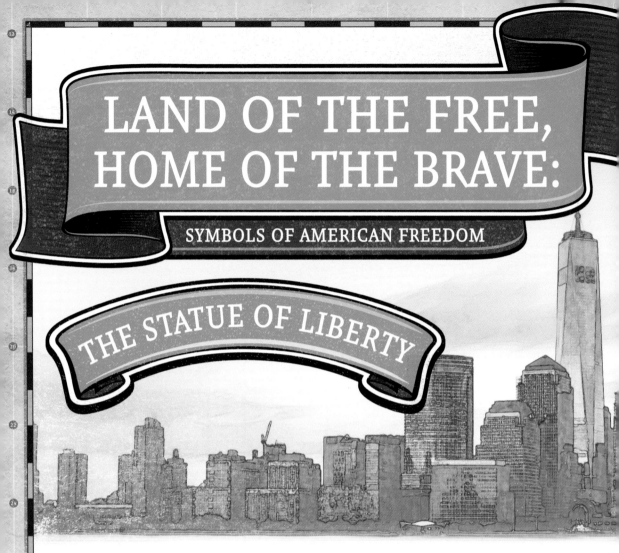

LAND OF THE FREE, HOME OF THE BRAVE:

SYMBOLS OF AMERICAN FREEDOM

THE STATUE OF LIBERTY

What landmark best represents America to you? For many people, the Statue of Liberty comes to mind. Lady Liberty is a symbol of freedom and hope worldwide. She has proudly stood on Liberty Island in New York Harbor since the French gifted her to the United States in 1886.

Frédéric-Auguste Bartholdi designed the huge sculpture, making sure that each element was meaningful. The spikes on the crown symbolize sun rays. The shackle and chains at the foot mark the end of slavery. The tablet that Lady Liberty holds is marked with the date of American independence: July 4, 1776.

FAST FACTS ABOUT THE STATUE

- *On windy days, the statue sways up to 3 inches (7.6 centimeters), and the torch sways up to 5 inches (12.7 centimeters)!*

- *The sculptor used his mother as a model for Lady Liberty.*

- *The poem on the statue's pedestal is by Emma Lazarus. The following line is known around the world: "Give me your tired, your poor, Your huddled masses yearning to breathe free . . ."*

ELLIS ISLAND

European immigrants, 1921

The historic Registry Room on Ellis Island

Ellis Island

Like the Statue of Liberty, Ellis Island is a well-known American landmark. Unless your family has American Indian ancestors, you are descended from immigrants. And for 62 years, many of those immigrants (more than 12 million) came through Ellis Island in New York Harbor.

Throughout history, the idea of becoming an American citizen has been a beacon of hope. Immigrants have come looking for work, education, religious freedom—a better life. This dream comes true for some people, but life in America can also be very challenging for immigrants.

To be allowed to enter the country, immigrants had to be in good health. If there was any sign of a contagious disease, an unlucky applicant could be denied entry. People were asked whether they had relatives already living here, how much money they had brought with them, and what work skills they had.

By the mid-1920s, only special cases were processed at Ellis Island, and, in 1954, it closed. The history of Ellis Island has insured that it will remain an American landmark and monument—the place where so many immigrants arrived filled with hope.

THE LIBERTY BELL

The Liberty Bell, which was originally hung at the Pennsylvania State House, may be best known for its infamous crack, which keeps it from being rung. The crack has been a part of the iconic bell since 1835, when it was said to have cracked while ringing for the funeral of a chief justice.

The Liberty Bell became a symbol for the **abolitionist** movement in the late 1830s. Like the bell, America at that time was divided and broken. After the Civil War, the bell traveled across the country as a symbol of freedom and unity. Later, a replica traveled the country to advance the cause of women's suffrage, or the right to vote.

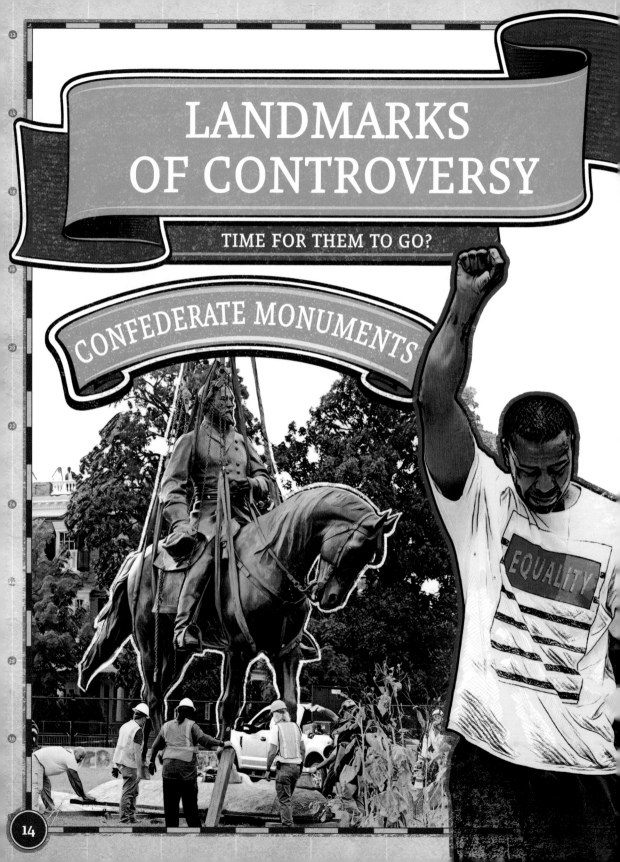

LANDMARKS OF CONTROVERSY

TIME FOR THEM TO GO?

CONFEDERATE MONUMENTS

You may have heard recent news stories about the removal of Confederate statues. These statues are monuments to Confederate soldiers and Civil War leaders. Protesters believe that they are symbols of racial injustice and the enslavement of Black people. Others feel that they are a piece of Southern culture and history.

More and more, Americans agree that Confederate monuments have no place in public areas, like parks. Statues should honor and remember the people they represent. But as Reverend Robert Lee IV (a descendant of the famous Confederate general Robert E. Lee) said, "Why are we protecting statues that symbolize oppression instead of protecting the people that were oppressed?"

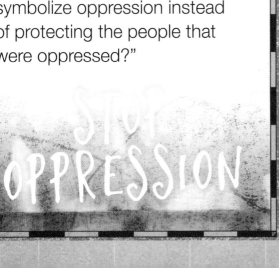

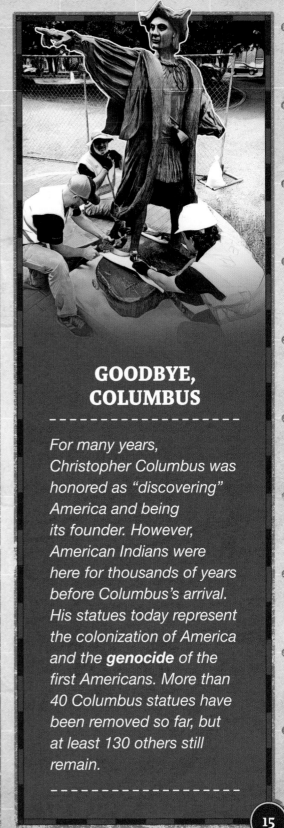

GOODBYE, COLUMBUS

*For many years, Christopher Columbus was honored as "discovering" America and being its founder. However, American Indians were here for thousands of years before Columbus's arrival. His statues today represent the colonization of America and the **genocide** of the first Americans. More than 40 Columbus statues have been removed so far, but at least 130 others still remain.*

Surprisingly, many Civil War statues were not erected right after the war. They were created nearly a hundred years later, during the civil rights movement of the 1960s. It was a time of great upheaval, when segregation was ending and minority groups were gaining rights. The purpose of the statues was to intimidate and scare Black people in the South.

While activists have fought for years to have offensive statues removed, the campaign grew stronger in the early 2020s with the **Black Lives Matter** movement. Some statues have been legally removed, while others have been toppled by frustrated protesters.

ANYONE NEED A STATUE?

What should be done with the offensive statues that are removed? In 2021, a statue of Robert E. Lee was taken down in Charlottesville, Virginia. A local museum of Black heritage has a creative idea of how to use it; they'd like to melt down the statue and use the bronze to create new, more inclusive artwork for the city.

PLACES TO REMEMBER

NATIONAL
SEPTEMBER 11 MEMORIAL

On September 11, 2001, the world was changed forever when terrorists flew two hijacked planes into the World Trade Center in New York City. Another plane was flown into the Pentagon, and passengers took down a fourth plane in Pennsylvania.

Where the Twin Towers used to stand, there are now two memorial pools where visitors can reflect and remember those who were lost on that day. The pools are giant—about an acre (.4 hectares) in size. Each waterfall flows down into a large hole that never fills up. The empty voids are symbolic of the loss our country experienced. The names of the victims are inscribed on **parapets**, or low walls, that surround the fountains.

NEVER
FORGET

SEPTEMBER 11,
2001

A PLACE OF REMEMBRANCE

The plaza around the pools is filled with more than 400 swamp white oaks, as well as a single pear tree. The special pear tree is known as the Survivor Tree. It was badly damaged during the attack but was nursed back to health and proudly stands in the plaza today—a symbol of **resiliency** *and hope.*

VIETNAM VETERANS

MEMORIAL

A visitor makes a rubbing of a loved one's name.

The Vietnam Veterans Memorial, located in Washington, DC, is an emotional place to visit. Two walls, each 246 feet (74.98 meters) in length, form a V made of black granite. They are inscribed with the names of approximately 58,000 people who were killed or were missing in action during the **controversial** war.

Visitors seem to feel compelled to touch the cool, smooth stone—a way to connect to the Americans who lost their lives in Vietnam. Some make rubbings of a name with paper and a piece of charcoal.

A WINNING DESIGN

Maya Lin was just a college senior when her design for "The Wall" was chosen from more than 1,400 submissions. Lin was majoring in architecture at Yale, but she had no professional experience. The submission was an assignment for a class. Lin received a B grade from her professor (who also entered the competition but obviously didn't win).

As World War II approached, anti-Asian feeling spread across the western United States. These feelings came to a peak in December of 1941, when Japanese forces bombed Pearl Harbor. Japanese immigrants, as well as Japanese Americans, were rounded up and forced into **incarceration camps** like the one in Manzanar, California. People were targeted only because of their race. They had to leave their homes, schools, jobs, and friends.

From 1942 to 1945, more than 10,000 people of Japanese descent were confined at Manzanar (and over 120,000 people were incarcerated across the West in all). The memorial tells their stories and bears witness to their pain and struggles.

WHAT TO LOOK FOR AT MANZANAR

If you visit Manzanar, it's important to know what to look for. Most of the structures are gone or have been buried, but remnants remain. You might see rock arrangements, water pipes, concrete foundations, sidewalks, and other artifacts—signs of life from decades ago. Like artifacts in a museum, these items are a part of history and can't be disturbed.

CHEROKEE TRAIL OF TEARS

The Cherokee people had lived in southern Appalachia for generations when White settlers began to move westward and push them out. By 1838, United States troops started rounding up the Cherokee and forcing them to leave their land.

The Trail of Tears, painted by Robert Lindneux in 1942

In total, about 16,000 Cherokee made the trek west to Oklahoma. They had very little clothing or provisions, and many died along the way. This path, or what remains of it, is known today as the Trail of Tears. It is part of the narrative of the Cherokee people, as well as a reminder of the unjust ways in which European settlers claimed someone else's land as their own.

John Ross, Cherokee Chief, protested the Treaty of New Echota

FORCED WEST

Sadly, the Cherokee were not the only American Indians to be displaced by President Jackson's policies, including the unjust Treaty of New Echota. Four other tribes—the Creek, Seminole, Chickasaw, and Choctaw—were also forced from their land and made to move west. The Cherokee Trail of Tears is the most well-known landmark, but similar paths also exist where about 90,000 people of other tribes had the same experiences.

NATURAL WONDERS

NIAGARA FALLS

American side of Niagara Falls

Visiting Niagara Falls on the border of the United States and Canada is a one-of-a-kind experience. Every second, 3,160 tons (2,867 metric tons) of water rush over the falls! Can you imagine the roar? The force of the water produces four million kilowatts of electricity, which is split between the United States and Canada.

Established in 1885 as a state park, Niagara Falls State Park is the oldest one in the United States. The falls themselves have been a work in progress much longer than that . . . for more than 12,000 years! When large quantities of ice melted after the last ice age, water flooded the Niagara River. The falls were formed as the water wore away at the **escarpment**.

Canadian side of Niagara Falls

A ride on the *Maid of the Mist* is a great way for visitors to see the Falls. It's also the wettest . . . every passenger gets a rain poncho!

THE EVERGLADES
NATIONAL PARK

One of the most remarkable things about the Everglades National Park in Florida is the variety of animals. More than 360 species of birds live in the swamps and wetlands, as well as manatees, bottlenose dolphins, alligators, crocodiles, 27 types of snakes, and even elusive Florida panthers!

In addition, a large variety of plants, including mangrove and cypress trees, sawgrass, and orchids, are found in this amazing 1.5-million-acre **ecosystem**. Today, the delicate balance of life in the Everglades is threatened—by pollution, human development, climate change, and **invasive species**. Preserving this landmark of the American landscape is vital. There is nowhere else like it in the world.

American Alligator

American Darter

Manatee

TRULY GRAND

Each year, nearly six million people visit the Grand Canyon in Arizona and marvel at its vibrant colors and awe-inspiring size. It's actually larger than Rhode Island! President Teddy Roosevelt made the Grand Canyon a national monument to protect it. He said, "Leave it as it is. You cannot improve on it. The ages have been at work on it, and man can only mar it."

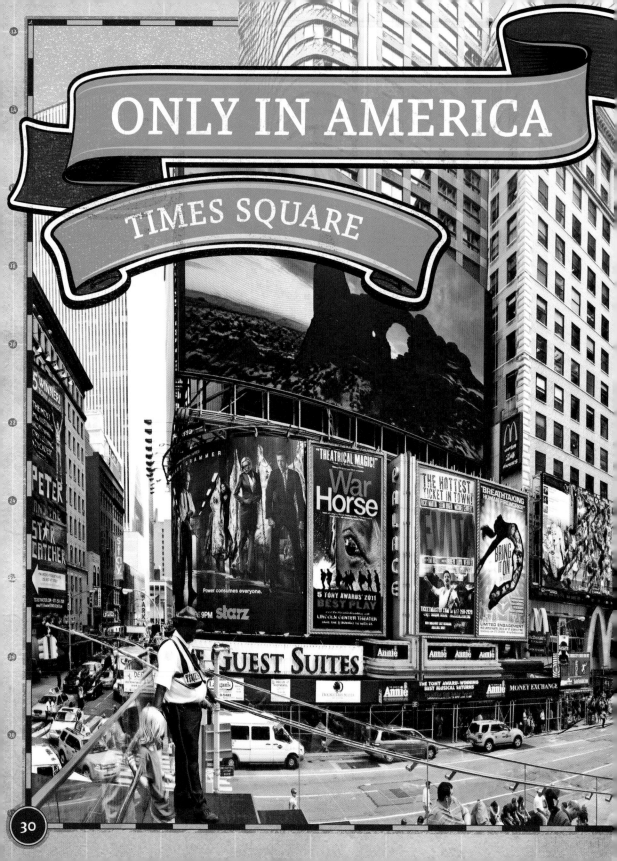

ONLY IN AMERICA

TIMES SQUARE

It's no wonder that Times Square is one of the most recognizable places on the planet. It's so bright, it can even be spotted from space! Times Square, in the heart of Manhattan, New York, was named in 1904 for the *New York Times* newspaper, which had its office there.

Times Square is the center of the well-known theater district in New York, including Broadway, where live shows (especially musicals) are performed. It's also the site of the famous ball drop on New Year's Eve. About 100,000 people come out each year to be a part of this televised event.

PIKE PLACE MARKET

Are you hungry for quail eggs, chocolate-dipped cherries, or pomegranate pepper jelly? Or maybe you're looking for homemade Greek yogurt, venison, or a peanut-butter-cup-stuffed cookie? If so, visit Pike Place Market, a Seattle, Washington, landmark since 1907.

The market has changed a lot over the years. In addition to produce, all kinds of meats, fish, cheeses, pastries, ethnic foods, and local crafts are sold here. The 9-acre (3.64-hectare) market hosts about 85 farmers, 240 vendors, and 225 craftspeople. If you want to do more than just visit, you're in luck—400 market apartments allow some people to call this landmark home.

Route 66 was proposed in 1925 as a series of connected interstate highways that would run across the western half of the nation. The eastern point of the route was Chicago, Illinois, and the western point was Santa Monica, California. It took until 1938 for the entire route to be paved, but it didn't take long for the famous highway to become known as the "Main Street of America."

Route 66 was built during the American fascination with the motor vehicle. Long-distance travel was becoming easier and more accessible. And nothing was more American than hitting the wide-open road.

ROUTE US 66

Mobilgas SPECIAL

REGULAR

Chicago

Bloomington

Springfield

Illinois

Missouri

St. Louis

Springfield

Tulsa

Oklahoma City

Oklahoma

Kansas

35

Because many people traveled long distances on Route 66, businesses sprang up in small towns along the way. Fast-food restaurants, motels, **roadside attractions**, and billboards all hoped to catch the attention (and the business) of traveling motorists.

Although you can still travel on parts of the old Route 66 today, much of it has been replaced by newer roads and superhighways. Even so, several businesses, museums, and tourist attractions still exist as a reminder of the best years of the famous American highway.

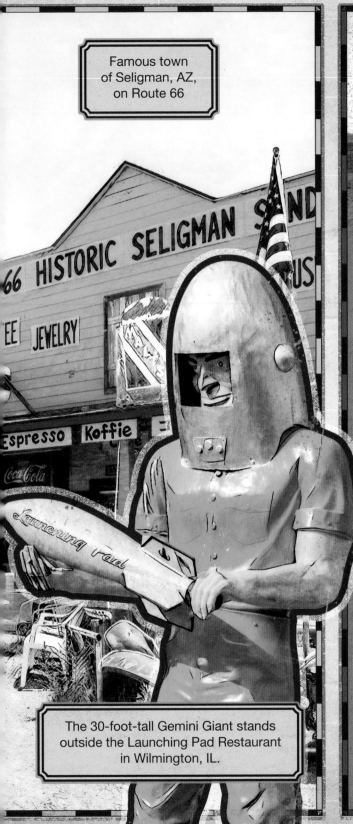

Famous town of Seligman, AZ, on Route 66

The 30-foot-tall Gemini Giant stands outside the Launching Pad Restaurant in Wilmington, IL.

WORTH A STOP ON ROUTE 66

- *Cadillac Ranch (Amarillo, TX): ten Cadillacs covered with graffiti, half buried in the ground*

- *Petrified Forest (Holbrook, AZ): the world's largest collection of petrified wood*

- *The Blue Whale (Catoosa, OK): a giant blue whale structure in a pond*

- *Blue Hole (Santa Rosa, NM): a bright blue swimming hole*

- *The Singing Road (Albuquerque, NM): when you drive over the rumble strips at 45 miles per hour (72.42 kilometers per hour), they play "America the Beautiful"*

AMAZING
ARCHITECTURE

HOOVER DAM

Hoover Dam is a concrete arch-gravity dam on the border of Arizona and Nevada. It dams the Colorado River and uses 17 generators to supply electricity to 100,000 homes! In addition, the dam helps prevent flooding and supplies drinking water and water for farm irrigation.

The creation of the dam, between 1931 and 1936, was a massive undertaking. More than 8.5 million pounds of dynamite were needed! Nearly one hundred men died during the construction, as well as the mascot dog, who is buried near the dam. The dam is 726 feet (221.29 meters) tall—more than twice as tall as the Statue of Liberty.

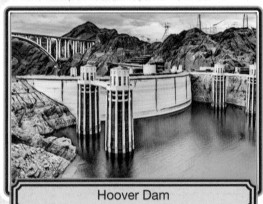

Hoover Dam

Hydroelectric turbines

A PART OF NATURE

Fallingwater, another water-centered landmark, was designed by architect Frank Lloyd Wright as a weekend home in Bear Run, Pennsylvania. The one-of-a-kind house was built to be an organic part of the landscape that surrounds it. It is built over a waterfall and even has a stairway from the living room to the stream below! Glass walls add to the feeling of being in a treehouse.

MESA VERDE

CLIFF DWELLINGS

For centuries, the Pueblo people of the American Southwest built their homes on the tops of **mesas**. Around 1190, they began to farm the tops of the mesas and build pueblos below the overhanging cliffs. At Mesa Verde National Park in Colorado, the remains of approximately 600 cliff dwellings are preserved.

The pueblos provide a glimpse into the lives of some of the first Americans. Artifacts show what their villages, food, and religious ceremonies might have been like. Unfortunately, looters and weathering have caused quite a bit of damage. But current preservation efforts mean that this monument to the Pueblo people will be around for generations.

ENTRANCE
MESA VERDE
NATIONAL PARK
U.S. DEPT. OF INTERIOR   NATIONAL PARK SERVICE

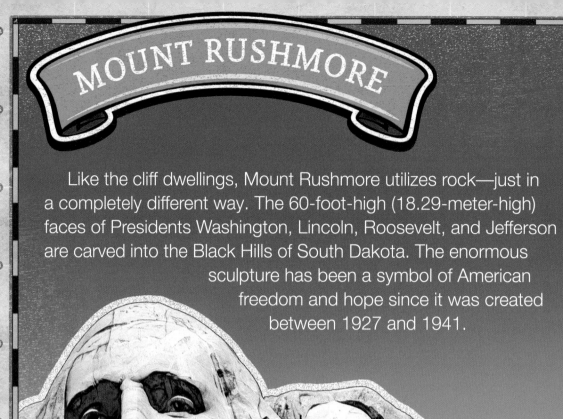

MOUNT RUSHMORE

Like the cliff dwellings, Mount Rushmore utilizes rock—just in a completely different way. The 60-foot-high (18.29-meter-high) faces of Presidents Washington, Lincoln, Roosevelt, and Jefferson are carved into the Black Hills of South Dakota. The enormous sculpture has been a symbol of American freedom and hope since it was created between 1927 and 1941.

Not everyone has the same views about the carvings, however. American Indians protested them right from the start because the land was sacred to the Lakota Sioux. They were the first residents of the area and were forced away from their land by White settlers.

GATEWAY ARCH

If heights don't make you queasy, you may want to visit the Gateway Arch in St. Louis, Missouri—the world's tallest arch at 630 feet, or 192 meters. (It's actually 630 feet wide too!) In the 1800s, the city was considered the "Gateway to the West" after the Louisiana Purchase and Lewis and Clark's famous expedition.

WE TRAVELED TO...

Find the location of each place you've traveled to while reading this book.

1. **Liberty Island/Ellis Island, NY**

2. **Manzanar, CA**

3. **Charlottesville, VA**

4. **Grand Canyon, AZ**

5. **Manhattan, NY**

6. **The Black Hills, SD**

7. **Bear Run, PA**

8. **Seattle, WA**

9. **Niagara Falls, NY**

10. **Route 66 (from Chicago, IL, to Santa Monica, CA)**

11. **Philadelphia, PA**

12. **Washington, D.C.**

13. **Mesa Verde, CO**

14. **Everglades National Park, South Florida**

15. **St. Louis, MO**

16. **Cherokee Trail of Tears**

17. **Hoover Dam, NV**

GLOSSARY

abolitionist (ab-uh-LISH-uh-nist): a person who believed in stopping slavery

Black Lives Matter (blak livz MA-tur): a movement that fights against racism and discrimination towards people of color

controversial (KAN-truh-VUHR-shul): causing disagreement

ecosystem (ee-koh-SIS-tuhm): a community of living things interacting with their environment

escarpment (ih-SKARP-muhnt): a steep slope or cliff

genocide (je-NUH-syde): an effort to get rid of all people belonging to a certain race or ethnic group

incarceration camp (in-kahr-suh-RAY-shuhn kamp): an area in which a group of people are confined unwillingly

invasive species (ihn-VAY-sihv SPEE-sheez): nonnative plants or animals that can cause harm to an ecosystem

mesas (MAY-suhs): pieces of land that are flat on top and have steep sides

parapets (PAE-ruh-pets): low walls or railings

resiliency (rih-ZIL-yuhn-see): the ability to recover from misfortune

roadside attractions (rohd-syde uh-TRAK-shunz): features alongside roads that are meant to catch the attention of tourists

INDEX

TEXT-DEPENDENT QUESTIONS

1. What is the historical importance of Ellis Island?

2. Why were many Civil War statues erected nearly a hundred years after the war?

3. Why were Japanese Americans sent to incarceration camps during World War II?

4. Explain why new businesses sprang up when Route 66 was built.

5. Name three current threats to the Everglades.

EXTENSION ACTIVITY

Design a landmark or monument for your town or city. For inspiration, think about the following: What do you love about where you live? What makes it unique? Does anyone famous live there? Does it have any natural features, like waterfalls or forests? Create a sketch, describe it in words, or create a brochure for future visitors.

BIBLIOGRAPHY

9/11 Memorial and Museum. Accessed October 12, 2021.
https://www.911memorial.org/.

ABC News. Accessed October 21, 2021.
https://abcnews.go.com/US/historians-debate-americas-sordid-history-racism-confederate-monuments/story?id=71486827.

Britannica, The Editors of Encyclopaedia. "Japanese American internment." Encyclopedia Britannica, June 3, 2021.
https://www.britannica.com/event/Japanese-American-internment.

Britannica, The Editors of Encyclopaedia. "Vietnam Veterans Memorial." *Encyclopedia Britannica*, September 15, 2017.
https://www.britannica.com/topic/Vietnam-Veterans-Memorial.

Green, Amanda Jackson. *Controversial Monuments: The Fight Over Statues and Symbols.* Minneapolis: Lerner Publishing Group, Inc., 2021.

National Park Foundation. Accessed October 14, 2021.
https://www.nationalparks.org/connect/blog/preservation-palace-mesa-verdes-cliff-dwellings.

National Park Service: History e-Library. Accessed October 13, 2021.
http://npshistory.com/publications/manz/index.htm.

Niagara Falls State Park. Accessed October 14, 2021.
https://www.niagarafallsstatepark.com/niagara-falls-state-park/amazing-niagara-facts.

The Statue of Liberty–Ellis Island Foundation, Inc.
Accessed October 11, 2021. https://www.statueofliberty.org/statue-of-liberty/overview-history/.

Lisa Kurkov is a freelance writer and editor who lives in North Carolina with her husband, two children, and a variety of animals. When her head isn't buried in a book, Lisa enjoys baking, crafting, photography, birding, and adventuring with her family. Her favorite US landmark is North Carolina's Cape Hatteras National Seashore.

www.rourkebooks.com

PHOTO CREDITS ©: Cover: Andrey_Kuzmin/ Shutterstock.com; Cover: Jennifer_Sharp/ Getty Images; Cover: Marco Rubino/ Shutterstock.com; Cover: Diego Grandi/ Shutterstock.com; Cover: michaeljung/ Getty Images; Page 1: MrsWilkins/ Getty Images; Page 1 ricorico/ Getty Images; Page 1: prochasson frederic/ Shutterstock.com; Page 4: titipongpwl/ Shutterstock.com; Page 5: darsi/ Shutterstock.com; Page 5: Joshua Janes; Page 5: f11photo/ Shutterstock.com; Page 5: jhshelton/ Shutterstock.com; Page 6: IM_photo/ Shutterstock.com; Page 6: Tavarius/ Shutterstock.com; Page 7: Belikova Oksana/ Shutterstock.com; Page 8: iofoto/ Shutterstock.com; Page: 8: Sean Pavone/ Shutterstock.com; Page 8: Everett Collection/ Shutterstock.com; Page 10: Everett Collection/ Shutterstock.com; Page 10: Everett Collection/ Shutterstock.com; Page 11: Everett Collection/ Shutterstock.com; Page 11: 19srb81/ Shutterstock.com; Page 12: Sean Pavone/ Shutterstock.com; Page 13: f11photo/ Shutterstock.com; Page 14: POOL/REUTERS/Newscom; Page 14: Bob Karp/ZUMA Press/Newscom; Page 15: F. Carter Smith/Polaris/Newscom; Page 16: Stephen Zenner/ ZUMAPRESS/Newscom; Page 17: Arthur B King/ Shutterstock.com; Page 19: ferrantraite/ Getty Images; Page 19: Regina Tolgyesi/ Getty Images; Page 19: Carl DeAbreu Photography/ Shutterstock.com; Page 20: Brandon Bourdages/ Shutterstock.com; Page 20: BONNIE CASH/UPI/Newscom; Page 21: Douliery Olivier/Sipa USA USA/Newscom; Page 22: JT Vintage/ZUMA Press/Newscom; Page 23: Stefan Wolny/ Shutterstock.com; Page 23: Circa Images / Glasshouse Images/Newscom; Page 24: Picture History/Newscom; Page 25: Glasshouse Images/Newscom; Page 26: Seumas Christie-Johnston/ Shutterstock.com; Page 27: Ruslan Kalnitsky/ Shutterstock.com; Page 28: John Apte/ Shutterstock.com; Page 29: RICIfoto/ Shutterstock.com; Page 29: Bildagentur Zoonar GmbH/ Shutterstock.com; Page 29: Harry Collins Photography/ Shutterstock.com; Page 29: sumikophoto/ Shutterstock.com; Page 30: Andrey Bayda/ Shutterstock.com; Page 32: f11photo/ Shutterstock.com; Page 32: Katae.Olaree/ Shutterstock.com; Page 33: Jianwei Zhu/ Shutterstock.com; Page 33: Checubus/ Shutterstock.com; Page 34: almir1968/ Getty Images; Page 34: Rainer Lesniewski/ Shutterstock.com; Page 34: Harry Kasyanov/ Shutterstock.com; Page 34: Ocskay Mark/ Shutterstock.com; Page 35: MrsWilkins/ Getty Images ; Page 35: Pernelle Voyage/ Shutterstock.com; Page 35: Thomas Bethge/ Shutterstock.com; Page 36: Jon Chica/ Shutterstock.com; Page 37: Nicola Patterson/ Shutterstock.com; Page 37: nick clephane/ Shutterstock.com; Page 38: Matej Hudovernik/ Shutterstock.com; Page 39: superjoseph/ Shutterstock.com; Page 39: Vlad G/ Shutterstock.com; Page 39: Vale Cantera/ Shutterstock.com; Page 40: milosk50/ Shutterstock.com; Page 41: Mia2you/ Shutterstock.com; Page 42: BeachfrontPhoto/ Shutterstock.com; Page 43: Oakley/ Shutterstock.com; Page various: LoudRedCreative/ Getty Images; Page various: Anna Timoshenko/ Shutterstock.com ; Page various: Miodrag Kitanovic/ Getty Images; Page various: Andrey_Kuzmin/ Shutterstock.com

Library of Congress PCN Data

U.S. Landmarks, Monuments, and Symbols / Lisa Kurkov

(Travel to...)

ISBN 978-1-73165-270-6 (hard cover)

ISBN 978-1-73165-234-8 (soft cover)

Library of Congress Control Number: 2021952197

ISBN 978-1-73165-300-0 (e-book)

ISBN 978-1-73165-330-7 (e-pub)

Rourke Educational Media

Printed in the United States of America

01-2412211937

Edited by: **Catherine Malaski**

Cover and interior design/illustration by: **Joshua Janes**